# Traveling, with Children:

## 10 Simple Tips For Making Travel a Pleasure

...for everyone

## D. N. Charles

# Traveling, with Children:
## 10 Simple Tips For Making Travel a Pleasure

### D. N. Charles

© D. N. Charles 2011

Published by 1stWorld Publishing
P.O. Box 2211, Fairfield, Iowa 52556
tel: 641-209-5000 • fax: 866-440-5234
web: www.1stworldpublishing.com

First Edition

LCCN: 2011911663
SoftCover ISBN: 978-1-4218-8616-9
eBook ISBN: 978-1-4218-8617-6

All rights reserved. No part of this book may be reproduced or utilized in any form or by any means, electronic or mechanical, including photocopying or recording, or by any information storage and retrieval system, without permission in writing from the author.

This material has been written and published solely for educational purposes. The author and the publisher shall have neither liability nor responsibility to any person or entity with respect to any loss, damage or injury caused or alleged to be caused directly or indirectly by the information contained in this book.

Mom, Dad, this is for you.

Thank you.

Babies don't have to be cranky—we simply have to know how to care for them.

# Being Comfortable While Traveling is Easy

We've all traveled by car, bus, train, and plane. The reasons could be for short trips, long journeys in and around the country, and overseas—as vacationers, tourists, college students, businesspeople, and more. When we travel, it's not unusual for us to encounter families with little infants and toddlers. How often on these travels have we come across families with young infants who are simply unhappy travelers, so unhappy that eventually their parents get frustrated and exhausted, making it difficult for fellow passengers to be comfortable as well?

These are times we want to put on the headphones and blast the music with maximum volume or wish someone had developed a technology to block sound out completely. Even the most adorable babies can become tiresome, with others passengers becoming increasingly impatient with restless unhappy infants. Babies don't have to be cranky—we simply have to know how to care for them.

A year ago my family took an overseas trip from O'Hare airport in Chicago to Frankfurt, Germany. It was an eight-hour flight. On that flight we got to experience the most common occurrence—an unhappy ☹ baby. She was as cute as a button, about nine months old, but extremely restless and very cranky. Her mother looked uncertain, slightly embarrassed, and a little nervous. It seemed like she was a first-time mom and her first experience traveling with her baby girl. After a few hours of listening, waiting, and watching, I turned around in my seat and asked if I could be of any assistance. The baby's mama was at this point very anxious and welcomed any suggestion I had. I offered a few tips. Sure enough, soon the baby settled down and eventually fell asleep for some time, only to wake up screaming when the plane began its decent. It was then that I decided to gather some points together for inexperienced parents traveling with infants.

As parents and fellow passengers, we don't want the experience of travel to be exhausting in any way, either because of our unhappy infant or another passenger's restless baby! Neither do we as parents want to start a journey or end a trip with a tired infant who has exhausted us and who has probably made other passengers uncomfortable. It's no fun to arrive at a destination and need to take the first few days recovering from the journey.

☹ ☹ ☹ ☹

I think most of us who are mothers loved playing pretend "mom" to dolls when we were little girls—gently brushing their hair and changing their clothes a zillion times a day, talking nonstop to them, taking them on walks, and caring for them in a gentle, loving fashion. That seemed to change as we grew up and began having our own little baby dolls for real! Now with our hectic schedules, we may sometimes take our babies for granted. Also, there is a common belief among some of us that babies don't have much awareness and don't know any better. Taking our children for granted and forgetting they are human too are the real causes for babies becoming discontent and cranky. This in turn makes parents impatient and they start finding it difficult to deal with their young ones. These situations occur even when we are not traveling.

So, during the journey, tensions build up from the restrictions of travel, our babies get cranky, and we as parents are struggling for what to do next. The simple guidelines provided here are to help parents, for whom it's the first time traveling with young ones. For experienced parents, these guidelines may serve as handy reminders.

As travelers, what do we do for ourselves before we embark on a journey? We dress thoughtfully and suitably, we pack with utmost detail and care.

Caring for ourselves should not be any different than

caring for our infants. They are people too—only very little people who are unable to communicate with words but can in other ways: smile ☺ when they are happy, sleep when they are content, and cry ☹ when they experience any form of discomfort.

The guidelines that follow will help us be prepared before our trip so we can travel as confident parents knowing our little ones are comfortable and content, and will not cause any distress for us or the fellow passengers. Always use your best judgment as a parent.

☹ ☹ ☹ ☹

# Dress Code

Moms and dads like to dress casually on trips. Take the same initiative for your infant. Dress your baby according to the length of the journey. Put the child in loose, easy-to-remove clothing. Babies like to feel free, with nothing constricting their movements. Avoid button-down clothing that will pinch your infant when on a seat or on his or her back in a bassinette. Dress the child in any soft clothing made with breathable fabric. Little girls do look pretty in dresses, hair clips, and hair bands, but those are not always the best on a journey. Baby boys do look adorable in jeans and jackets, but are they really soft and comfortable clothing for travel? Choosing the right apparel is the first step.

# Weather/Temperature Control

The climate is a major factor as well. If it is cold, make sure the child is bundled up outside; once inside, however, be aware of the airport or airplane cabin temperature. With the same outside apparel, the baby could get too hot and fidgety. On a summer vacation, although it's hot outside, the air-conditioning in airports and plane cabins do get rather chilly, so a light sweater would be appropriate. Sometimes even cotton socks are required. Make sure you travel with a light cover of some sort. One can usually tell by touching the baby's hands and feet whether he or she is cold or hot. If the child's hands and feet are cold, then a light blanket or some cover might be needed. If the face is red, then your baby is too hot and it's time to remove some clothing.

# Comfort

Whether at the airport or on the plane, make your baby as physically comfortable as possible. Sometimes when we first arrive at the airport there is a wait for a certain length of time before we get on the airplane or a layover waiting for a connecting flight. If the baby is already in a stroller or cramped, the child will feel worse when it's time to board the aircraft. So, find a spot where you can spread a blanket down and let your baby kick up his or her heels, let them get a little action! This short period of exercise will probably make it easier for the baby to settle down once confined to a crib, lap, or seat. Please remember to check the diapers, if you have time before you board the plane. Babies don't like soggy diapers, so this will be something to do every couple of hours.

# Seat Allocation

If your plane journey is going to be longer than a couple of hours on the bigger planes and you know well in advance that you will be making this trip with your baby, then try to arrange with your airline for a bassinette. Ask for a seat up front where the airline provides the option to put up a bassinet or crib. This will give the baby room to stretch around and give you a chance to get some rest from holding your baby for the entire journey. While the plane is cruising at its desired altitude and if you have managed to get a seat in front near the exits, you can ask a crew member if it's appropriate to put your baby down on a blanket if there is enough leg room for you to do so; this again is helpful for when the baby is active.

# Takeoff, Landing, and Turbulence

Just like us, our babies have difficulty during take off and landing. The best way to start the trip is to have a content baby. Babies traveling with a slight cold can suffer much discomfort during a flight. It is suggested that you nurse your baby during takeoff and especially landing as the latter seems to have a greater effect on the ears rather than when the plane gains altitude. Carry a bottle with water, milk, or even juice; have it ready to give it to the baby when you start to feel the pressure. If the child is a bit older and teething, this would be a good time to give him or her a chewy snack, which will help pop the ears. During turbulence, if the baby is restless, hold your baby and again nurse or feed her or him. Long-distance travel is the time for you to request your pediatrician to prescribe a remedy that will help your baby rest in case of a cold, cough or colic. This will also help during takeoff and landing, which can be extremely painful to infants and young children.

# Hydration

Keeping the baby well hydrated is quite important, which is something we occasionally forget. Airplane atmosphere can be very dehydrating. Travel usually is tiring and seems to feel worse when one is dehydrated. Try to avoid anything that is sweet. Too much juice can cause more colic from gas and wind in the stomach, which will make the baby cranky. Lukewarm or room temperature water and milk is very helpful. Because you are keeping the baby hydrated, naturally the diapers will need to be monitored more often. This is a common cause for baby discomfort—soggy, full diapers. ☹

# Entertainment

Carry five to six toys with you. Bring ones that are interactive like soft books made out of fabric or a bendable toy—something they can twist or chew on. Preferably noiseless toys that are bright, colorful, and easy for the baby to grasp. The trick here is to give it to your child one at a time. When the baby gets restless, give her or him one toy only. Take the first one away, then hand the child the second; this keeps him or her fascinated and distracted for longer. If the baby is able to sit up and look at the monitor in front, there are always cartoons playing on international flights that are a great form of distraction for all ages. ☺

# Interaction

Your baby has probably never seen so many people in such a small space. It can make an infant insecure to have this many strangers around. Perhaps you can chat with your neighbor to let the baby feel a little more at ease. Talk to your baby—sometimes all the child needs to hear is a parent's soothing voice. Use a tone that makes the child know you understand his or her discomfort and dilemma. Even though children may not understand what you are saying, they listen and like to hear their parents' voices so interact with your baby with a patient, caressing tone. Also, it's OK to get up and walk the aisle with your child, once the food has been served and the aisle is clear. When you make an effort, the baby senses that and knows you are reaching out and care.

# Rest

We all need our rest and sleep. If you and the baby can get a couple of hours sleep on the plane, then both of you will be happier guests at your final destination. These days there are a number of herbal and homeopathic supplements to give babies. Always talk with your pediatrician or health practitioner before any supplement is given; perhaps the doctor can also recommend something suitable for your baby. This maybe one of those times you would like to use these supplements for comfortable and easy travel.

# Timing

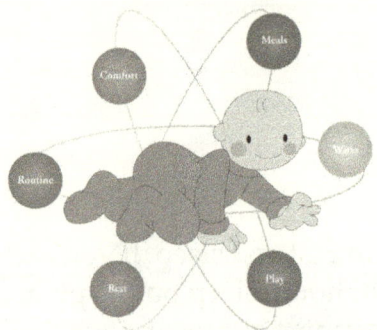

On long international flights, we should keep in mind the routine and timings for your baby. It's best to stick to the routine the child is used to. Try to feed them according to the timing at home. If it's milk every three hours, then its best to do the same on flight. Keeping to the routine will also help the baby feel a sense of familiarity rather than change, which is not always welcome in strange surroundings.

These guidelines are for parents with infants and younger children. They are some of the ways to become more aware of your child's needs and maintain harmony.

# Older Children

Of course with older children the options are plenty. If we don't want to be solely dependent on electronics, then the old-fashioned system of entertainment can always be used: coloring books, puzzles, easy-to-carry travel games, like chess, snakes, and shoots/ladders card games. One good idea that is also educational is a simple pair of binoculars! A window seat would be great. Just get your child to look out and make a list of what he or she has seen. Have the child to keep a journal. This is something the child can have as a keepsake or share with friends and teachers in school. There are so many ways to entertain older children if we as parents take the initiative and make a little effort.

# Conclusion

All in all, these are the main points we must remember to make traveling more enjoyable for ourselves and our little ones.

We must learn to understand our baby's needs which are really quite simple. Comfort is the key factor.

We need to ask ourselves, "Are they too cold or too hot?" "Are the clothes appropriate for travel?" "Is their diaper full, stomach empty, perhaps they are in need of some water?"

Another way to keep your children content is by remembering they enjoy a routine.

By giving your child a schedule with some repetition, they become familiar and comfortable with daily events and feel safe and secure. Regular timing for meals and bedtime greatly contributes to a child's level of contentment.

Very often, in unfamiliar surroundings, they may simply need just a little more affection, interaction, entertainment, or a distraction from their discomfort.

As kids, we have all traveled with our parents, and now as adults we continue this tradition with our own children. With a little thought, effort, care, and most importantly, love, our infants/toddlers grow up as happy children.

Have a safe and pleasant adventure! ☺

www.ingramcontent.com/pod-product-compliance
Lightning Source LLC
Chambersburg PA
CBHW051720040426
42446CB00008B/984